YOUR KNOWLEDGE HAS VALUE

- We will publish your bachelor's and master's thesis, essays and papers

- Your own eBook and book -
  sold worldwide in all relevant shops

- Earn money with each sale

Upload your text at www.GRIN.com
and publish for free

Bibliographic information published by the German National Library:

The German National Library lists this publication in the National Bibliography; detailed bibliographic data are available on the Internet at http://dnb.dnb.de .

This book is copyright material and must not be copied, reproduced, transferred, distributed, leased, licensed or publicly performed or used in any way except as specifically permitted in writing by the publishers, as allowed under the terms and conditions under which it was purchased or as strictly permitted by applicable copyright law. Any unauthorized distribution or use of this text may be a direct infringement of the author s and publisher s rights and those responsible may be liable in law accordingly.

Imprint:

Copyright © 2017 GRIN Verlag
Print and binding: Books on Demand GmbH, Norderstedt Germany
ISBN: 9783668613935

This book at GRIN:

https://www.grin.com/document/387310

Kaia Smith

What value does Marxism have in analyzing contemporary inequality?

GRIN Verlag

GRIN - Your knowledge has value

Since its foundation in 1998, GRIN has specialized in publishing academic texts by students, college teachers and other academics as e-book and printed book. The website www.grin.com is an ideal platform for presenting term papers, final papers, scientific essays, dissertations and specialist books.

Visit us on the internet:

http://www.grin.com/

http://www.facebook.com/grincom

http://www.twitter.com/grin_com

What value does Marxism have in analyzing contemporary inequality?

Kaia Smith

Essay submitted to the International Inequalities Institute, London School of Economics

18 January 2017

"Billionaires getting richer doesn't mean someone else getting poorer." Such reads the headline of one of the top Google News search results for "Oxfam", the organization which earlier this week released a report with statistics highlighting the unprecedented degree of global inequality. One of them is that eight billionaires have the same wealth as half of the world's population. The author, writing for the IB Times UK, does not engage with any of the report's other staggering statistics, such as: 21 million people are forced laborers, generating an estimated $150 billion in profits each year; 1/3 of the world's billionaires' wealth is inherited, while 43% can be linked to cronyism; $7.6 trillion of wealth is hidden in offshore tax-havens (Oxfam International, 2017). Rather, he claims that "all these people have created jobs, paid lots in taxes, and in the case of Bill Gates donated tens of billions of dollars to charity" (Bowman, 2017) and explains that 'extreme poverty' and basic indicators of well-being have been shown to be steadily improving. The article offers thereby an orthodox explanation to why the working class supports, or at least accepts, a system that leaves them at the bottom of the socio-economic hierarchy: because it, too, profits; because wealth trickles down. As the Panama Papers have shown, however, and Oxfam and other research groups support that observation, wealth does not trickle down – it merely moves offshore (Henry, 2012). In this essay, however, I will argue that (Gramscian) Marxism helps us to uncover the systemic and epistemic conditions that create and reproduce inequalities by critically reflecting on the exploitative mechanisms that govern them and the institutionalized hegemonic power discourses that naturalize exploitation. It is therefore apt to debunk 'trickle-down' as the neoliberal elite narrative that it is and to place the working class individual, and its communal and class self-awareness, at the center of a solution to inequality. In order to do that, I will first sketch the exploitative nature of the capitalist mode of production to attain an economic foundation for a socio-cultural argument and then show that Gramscian cultural hegemony theory offers a more compelling explanation for the persistence of such a capitalist logic premised on exploitation, with no effective resistance by those which are exploited under it.

The study of inequality today has emerged in response to the unprecedented extent of socioeconomic polarization. Thus far, those advocating for the curtailment of inequalities have had to make their case in stark opposition to pervasively established neoliberal ideology, which values a free, deregulated global economy and the unrestrained accumulation of capital. In order to do this, positivist approaches that link common practices to patterns of disadvantage have highlighted a myriad of processes showing that inequalities persist and accumulate. However, in this paper I will challenge the notion that such atomized processes are simply the 'symptoms' of the 'disease' of inequality; rather, using theories of exploitation as a tool, I argue that inequality is the symptom of a more vast disease: capitalism, especially in its contemporary financial form. While positivist approaches are integral to understanding and finding solutions to the most unjust of inequalities, theories of exploitation allow us to think about the systemic conditions in which knowledge about inequalities is produced and negotiated, and are thereby able to uncover a broader, deeper, and more fundamental socio-economic narrative which guides the actions and even ideologies of each person implicated in its production process. In order to make these claims, I define a "theory of exploitation" as a general Marxist approach, with some neo-Marxist considerations, while relying mainly on Gramscian Marxism (hegemony theory). Assuming that the "analysis of inequality" is mostly intended to alleviate them, I consider its current state to be multifaceted and vast beyond my personal scope, but generally positivist and pro-market. Further, I will consider both social and economic inequalities, as if Marxism and Gramscianism are indeed 'valuable', that is useful, additions, they should offer an increased capacity to alleviate inequalities when incorporated into mainstream social and economic analytic approaches. For the purpose of this essay, I will use Wright's definition of exploitation as a relationship of interdependence based on three notions: the material well-being of exploiters is taken at the expense of the other group, resulting in material harm of the exploited; in order to do this, the exploited experience restricted access to productive resources; this exclusion from resources leads to material advantage to exploiters as they own the labor effort of the exploited (Wright, 2005, 24). Although acknowledging sub-complexities, I thereby assume a generally binary class system for the purposes of this paper, consisting of the elite, business, or capitalist class, and the working class, or majority.

Economic Exploitation

Marxism claims that that well-being cannot be realized without eradicating the free market, as it is predicated upon and sustained by a binary system of exploitation of the proletariat by the bourgeoisie. It further emphasizes the implication of capitalist control over the means of production, which takes the product of the worker's labor away from himself, dissociating him from the appreciation of his own creation. This alienates the worker from himself, the material world, and the capitalist that owns his production. Moreover, the capitalist takes away the worker's power over the value of his labor, then imbues it with additional value for sale on the market and keeps all surplus value. In the accumulation of money, bar government regulation, he is restrained only by competition in the marketplace and therefore seeks to maximize exploitation-based profit at all costs (Marx, 1845). Marxism claims that this exploitative process systematically hinders individuals from exercising their agency, and that it can do so in surreptitious ideological ways which may blind members of the working class to their exploitee status.

Notable trends in developing countries undergird the importance of understanding the principle of exploitation and its effects. After all, wealth tends to accumulate faster than growth, and there is no feature inherent to capitalism that would stop this accumulation from continuing (Piketty, 2014). Additionally, monopolistic tendencies have increased, giving more market power than ever before to the largest of firms; again, this is partly brought about by the inherent efficiency grounded in free-market capitalism (Taylor, 2016; Baran and Sweezy, 1966; Stiglitz, 2016b). Declines in unionization have taken place in many industrialized economies, notably the US and the UK (Economist, 2015). Financial institutions have not been shown to increase productivity despite an increase in CEOs' share of national incomes; furthermore, this has happened amidst stagnation of median wages (Stiglitz, 2016a). This economic polarization of wealthy and majority induces a number of social, cultural, and political disadvantages (Hills and Cunliffe, 2016), including increased class polarization (Savage, 2015). How does all of this relate to exploitation? Firstly, as the Oxfam report shows, there is massive tax avoidance in the face of increasing wealth, which leads to decreased social benefits for the majority. Increased monopoly power means, among other things, higher barriers to market entry for smaller firms and decreased consumer agency. Disempowered unions signal an imbalance of power in employment relations. Lastly, lowered productivity while median wages stagnate indicates that the business class, on average, is working less and earning more while the majority works more and earns less. Thereby, all of these trends, and their implications, are compatible with exploitation.

Cultural hegemony

According to Marx, the mode of production determines the character of social, intellectual, and cultural life. Having just discussed how capitalist patterns affect the majority, let us now think about the cultural and power relations behind them. Even with economics as the basis for all other cultural processes (Bourdieu, 1986), contemporary accumulation processes do not require overt exploitation (Savage, 2015). Furthermore, power relations concern the ways in which activities are controlled, not simply the distribution of resources. This leads us to an important and puzzling question: *How is this exploitative system tolerated by the majority who may lose out?*

Gramsci's theory of cultural hegemony (1971) provides us an indispensable tool with which to attempt an answer. He views mass culture as an instrument used by the elite class to maintain political and social control through the production of ideological 'false consciousness.' Mainly through the media (and other institutions that affect reality perceptions such as schools and organizations), ideological values are disseminated for the reproduction of elite power domination. Their henceforth ubiquity can partially explain the naturalization, or inoculation, of values that are in the interest only of capitalists, to the majority. However, he also ascribes latent power to subaltern groups. If they harness that power and create their own culture, they can assert their dominance and potentially become the cultural hegemon. Thus his approach has Marxist underpinnings, as he advocated a working-class takeover of the capitalist state, but he takes a less deterministic approach to a change in power relations. Gramsci rightly emphasizes the importance of analyzing ideology at the level of the 'superstructure,' or the cultural, social, and political manifestations of the economic base of society, rather than individual, atomized movements or events, thus looking at the bigger picture of society and the potential for positive change.

Theoretically, Gramsci's approach offers an open-minded and constructivist outlook, which when analyzing the structural source of inequalities is an indispensable addition to a largely positivist field unable to explain the contradiction between contemporary capitalism's persistence and worker exploitation. By looking more broadly at the social and economic context in which this contradiction takes place, Gramscianism allows us to analyze its sources and, by recognizing and encouraging the agency of the majority in balancing socioeconomic power relations, find novel solutions to it. After all, economic and social orders are not magical; rather they are of our own creation. Gramscianism urge the majority to therefore take back their agency within the social structure, rather than being convinced of 'freedom' by elite ideology.

Practically, this theory helps us to understand contemporary capitalism's persistence – partly due to the lack of resistance and even support of the working class -- because it focuses on the broader structural influence behind the social and economic exchanges that end up (re)producing inequalities. It is particularly the mass media that reify and institutionalize that process. Increasing economic inequalities have also polarized the ability to own and influence media and the ideology contained in its messages; in fact, concentration of media ownership has continued to accumulate over time; for example, in 1983, 90% of US mass media was controlled by fifty companies; today, 90% is controlled by just six (Lutz, 2012). Additionally, linkages in the mass media to the general business class have increased (Chomsky and Herman, 2006). That advertising is the primary income source of media outlets indicates that cultural dissemination is primarily profit-driven, serving the interests of those providing the funds, and thereby influencing media prosperity and survival, rather than the majority of the public (ibid., 266-7). The concentration of media control has placed the power to disseminate culture and therefore ideology in the hands, once again, of a privileged few. Furthermore, as Herman and Chomsky say, "in a world of concentrated wealth and major conflicts of class interest, to fulfill this role requires systematic propaganda" (2006, 257).

This understanding, which is related to Marx and Gramsci's notion of 'false consciousness,' or the state of being inhibited from perceiving the exploitative nature of one's economic and/or social situation (Marx 1845, Gramsci 1992), paves the way to answer the underlying puzzle: how exploitation can persist despite it being of disinterest to the exploited. Bourdieu's concept of 'misrecognition' is similar; he notes that as the arbitrariness of entitlements for power and privileges becomes more apparent, those in dominant positions must invest more of their resources in disguising this arbitrariness to maintain dominance (Bourdieu, 1986). The vagueness of the term 'exploitation' itself can serve the interests of the elite class and therefore disguise itself. For example, the US mass media's efforts to attribute the positively connoted term 'job creators' with the super wealthy shrouds the fact that many of them are hiding their wealth in tax havens rather than contributing to public funds. Although the mass media representing the business class does enjoy a strong imbalance of power in its favor, the distribution of its messages is also a social process in which those with less power can internalize and discuss with others; this naturalizes both the mass media's power and its ideology through its ubiquity in social relations (Couldry, 2000). To use Burawoy's (2012) analogy, workers in capitalism are like chess players in a chess game: there would no longer be any point in playing if the individuals were to question the legitimacy of the system's rules. As in a game of chess, workers are given a sense of purpose to distract them from their exploited condition through, notably, the possibility of promotions with which to navigate the hierarchy of the workplace. Such institutionalization of values means that it does not simply require actions of the business class to disseminate capitalist ideology; it can, furthermore, be reproduced through social relations of the majority. In order to attain social mobility, individuals may even disadvantage members of their common class in situations of competition in order to 'get ahead' (Lamont et al, 2014, 22).

It is important to link micro-cognitive and macro-level processes in such a way to show how social interactions and cultural information allow individuals to make sense of reality, and eventually make the [re]production of inequality routine, intentionally or unintentionally (Lamont et al, 2014). The link between these two realms allows us to see how exploitation can operate at both the conscious/rational and the unconscious/systemic levels. The consistent application of universal rules and norms over time can start to be perceived as neutral simply due to their historic institutionalization. For example, even though standardized testing in the US was designed to increase social mobility, it reinforced inequality because the education process required to pass it was unequal itself (Lamont et al, 2014, 20). This example, along with many other instances of failed policies to alleviate inequalities, highlights the need to focus on changing structural issues, e.g. changes to educational practices that necessitate zero-sum educational outcomes, rather than atomized relationships of exclusion.

Together, these patterns suggest that both individual illusionment of a system and its legitimation through historical repetition are important concepts to understanding why workers may tolerate and uphold an exploitative society. This brings me to my final point regarding the value of exploitation theory to contemporary inequalities: Marxism highlights the empowerment of the exploited, and Gramscianism in particular emphasizes the need for them to acquire the discursive, intellectual, and practical means to understand their situation and redress it.

Despite the important shift in focus that the aforementioned contributions Marxism and Gramscianism can offer to the study of inequalities, they certainly include many assumptions and gaps. Notably, the task of overthrowing a global socioeconomic ideology is overwhelming, if not impossible, and without a positive, practical theory of an alternative, these approaches do not seem up to said task. As mentioned before, the term 'exploitation' is ambiguous, which is not necessarily to capitalism's detriment; to simultaneously recognize the ability of all actors to obtain increased power others through social process and to assume that greedy and unjust tendencies are inherent in an entire social system seems lazily pessimistic about humanity in general. Nonetheless, the value of 'zooming out' outweighs, as it allows us to observe and critically think about the structures in which we are embedded and thereby constitutes an integral tool to solving the problem of inequalities today; at a time when the outcomes of wealth inequality are so radical that eight people have as much financial power as 3.6 billion, there is a need for radical solutions. Properly pointing out and justly prescribing the massive and increasing failings of our contemporary system of capitalism is necessary as it becomes more unsustainable. We should not avoid discussing the possibility of collectively negotiating a more equitable society in which we justify the terms amongst ourselves rather than submit to a system that does not care for our fulfillment let alone our well-being, just because it is utopian.

In conclusion, I have argued that theories of exploitation, particularly of cultural hegemony, add value to analyzing contemporary social and economic inequalities in three ways: first, Marxism urges us to step outside the ontological realm of contemporary capitalism to look critically at the system of production we inhabit, and question whether its structure is societally equitable and sustainable. Secondly, Gramscianism asks us to further question the ideologies that consolidate and reproduce social and economic relations, rather than focusing solely on how these isolated processes produce inequalities. Accordingly, mainstream media institutions, largely funded by the elite, not only fail to represent the interests of the majority of the global population, but they 'seduce' us into accepting values of consumerism and social mobility so that we 'consent' to sustaining the neoliberal capitalist mode of production. This constitutes a form of ideological exploitation which deprives a majority of people from representation, community, self-awareness, and empowerment, and induces them to continue to supply their labor and demand to a market that does not ensure equitable distribution of resources for adequate human flourishing. Thirdly, these approaches bring attention to the importance of collective awareness and action in the face of confronting the economic system and its associated ideology. In order to solve the vast issue of inequalities today, the 'working class' need a sense of community and empowerment in order to renegotiate a new system of production which serves the needs and interests of all and not, above all, the wealthiest eight men on the planet.

References

Baran, P. A., & Sweezy, P. M. (1966) *Monopoly capital: An essay on the American economic and social order*. New York, NY: Monthly Review Press.

Bourdieu, P. (1986) The forms of Capital. In Richardson, J. *Handbook of theory and research for the sociology of education*. New York, NY: Greenwood Press.

Bowman, Sam (2017, January 16) Billionaires getting richer doesn't mean someone else getting poorer. *International Business Times UK*. Retrieved from www.ibtimes.co.uk

Burawoy, M. (2012). The Roots Of Domination: Beyond Bourdieu And Gramsci. *Sociology, 46*(2), 187-206.

Couldry, N. (2000). *The place of media power: Pilgrims and witnesses of the media age*. London: Routledge.

Durham, M.G. and Kellner, D. (2006) Introduction. In Durham, M.G. and Kellner, D. (eds.), *Media And Cultural Studies: Keyworks*. (i-xxxviii). Malden, MA: Blackwell.

The Economist (2015, September 28) Why Trade Unions Are Declining. Retrieved from www.economist.com

Gottdiener,M . (1985). Hegemony and Mass Culture: A Semiotic Approach. *American Journal of Sociology, 90* (5), 979-1001.

Gramsci, A., In Hoare, Q., & In Nowell-Smith, G. (1971). Selections from the prison notebooks of Antonio Gramsci. New York: International Publishers.

Henry, J. (2012) The Price of Offshore Revisite: New estimates for "missing" global private wealth, income, inequality, and lost taxes. *Tax Justice Network.*

Herman, E. and Chomsky, N. (2006) A Propaganda Model. In Durham, M.G. and Kellner, D. (eds.), *Media And Cultural Studies: Keyworks*. (257-294). Malden, MA: Blackwell.

Hills, J. & Cunliffe, J. (2016) Accumulated Advantage and Disadvantage: The Role of Wealth. In Dean, H. & Platt, L. (eds) *Social Advantage and Disadvantage*. (161-178). Oxford: Oxford University Press.

Horkheimer, M. & Adorno, T. W. (2006) The Culture Industry: Enlightenment as Mass Deception. In Durham, M.G. and Kellner, D. (eds.), *Media And Cultural Studies: Keyworks*. (41-72). Malden, MA: Blackwell.

Lamont, M., Stefan B., & Clair, M. (2014). What is Missing? Cultural Processes and Causal Pathways to Inequality. *Socio-Economic Review*, 1-36.

Lutz, A. (2012, June 14)These 6 Corporations Control 90% Of The Media In America. *Business Insider*. Retrieved from www.businessinsider.com

Marx, K. (1845) *The German Ideology, with F. Engels* [Republished in D. McLellan (ed.) (1977) *Karl Marx, Selected Writings*, Oxford University Press: Oxford].

Oxfam International. (2017) An Economy For The 99%. Oxford: Oxfam GB.

Piketty, T., & Goldhammer, A. (2014) *Capital in the twenty-first century*. Cambridge, Massachusetts: The Belknap Press of Harvard University Press.

Savage, M. (2015) Introduction to elites: From the 'problematic of the proletariat' to a class analysis of 'wealth elites.' *The Sociological Review 63*(2), 223-239.

Savage, M., Warde, A. & Devine, F. (2005) Capitals, assets and resources: some critical issues. *The British Journal of Sociology 56*(1), 31-47.

Stiglitz, J. (2016a) Inequality and Economic Growth. In Jacobs, M. & Mazzucato, M. (eds.) *Rethinking Capitalism: An Introduction*. Wiley-Blackwell.

Stiglitz, J. (2016b) Monopoly's New Era. *Project Syndicate*. Retrieved from www.projectsyndicate.org

Taylor, S. (2016, May 16) Rising monopoly power may partly explain US inequality and productivity slowdown. Retrieved from www.simontaylorsblog.com/2016/05/16/rising-monopoly-power-may-partly-explain-us-inequality-and-productivity-slowdown

Wright, E. O. (2005) Foundations of a neo-Marxist class analysis. In Wright, E.O. (ed.), *Approaches to Class Analysis* (4-30). Cambridge: Cambridge University Press.

YOUR KNOWLEDGE HAS VALUE

- We will publish your bachelor's and
  master's thesis, essays and papers

- Your own eBook and book -
  sold worldwide in all relevant shops

- Earn money with each sale

Upload your text at www.GRIN.com
and publish for free